Fifteen Grades of Hay

DEREK THE WEATHERSHEEP

Thankyou for being part of
'team Bride' and for making
my hen weekend one that will
'NEVER' be forgotten.

As a tribute to 15 hens on a
farm and one Buff Butler Called
Chrishan . . . .

I give you this book!

With much love

Caz
xxo

ISBN-10: 148025407X
ISBN-13: 978-1480254077

DEDICATION

This book is dedicated to all my followers on Facebook and Twitter. You really do brighten up each and every one of my days. Thank you one and all. Derek x

www.weathersheep.com

CONTENTS

PREFACE

Although Derek the Weathersheep has his name on the front of the book, I would like to point out that this is my story, told in my own words. Derek has kindly lent me his name for the purposes of the book so that we can reach his huge following.

I hope you enjoy it.

Dolly the Weathersheep.

1 A PARTY

I bleat with anger at my fleece. Damn my woolly locks. They just won't behave and damn Brenda for not letting me use her new fleece shampoo, especially the one formulated for flyaway fleeces.

Brenda is my barn-mate and has been for several years. A Cardiff girl, she's been around the block a bit. My best friend, she's the girl I can usually rely on. But today she's got the shits. Big time. One slight cough and the barn ain't going to smell too good.

The trouble is, is that she is supposed to be coming with me to the party in the farmhouse today. It is a sunny Easter Saturday afternoon. Farmer Honey and his wife are heading down to the market today so the girls do what they usually do when the house is empty and use the place for a knees-up. I guess I'm just going to have to go on my own.

"I'm sorry Dolly love. It's just my guts aren't feeling too good you know? They seem to be mulching over and over and I can't go sinking Rich Tea biscuits with the state I'm in. You'll be ok. The other girls are nice enough."

"I guess so." I say. "It's just that I've always been to parties with you in the past."

"Go on. Have a few biscuits for me eh? I'm just going to stay here in the barn with a cork up my arse."

I pop some lipstick on and head out across the field to the farmhouse. By the time I get there, the party is already in full swing. I pass a girl on my way in, stood at the back door. She's part of Chain Command. She's there to alert us when Farmer Honey comes back. There are two other girls – the first one is stood at the end of the field that overlooks the valley and the road leading up to the house. When she first sees Farmer Honey's Land Rover, she signals to one of the other girls, who is stood in the middle of the field. She then alerts the girl stood at the back door, who's already looking a bit worse for wear.

"You shouldn't be eating biscuits on duty." I say to her as I open the back door. She ignores me and I step inside.

There are girls everywhere. Empty Hobnob packets litter the living room and biscuit barrels lie empty on the floor. I can hardly hear myself think above the sound of S Club 7 and I push my way towards the kitchen. I've never seen a party this wild. I just wish that Brenda was by my side. I'd feel a lot better if she was.

"Hobnob?" I get a chocolate biscuit shoved in my face.

"No thanks." I didn't want to go straight for the hard stuff. "Got a Malted Milk?" A girl rummages around in a biscuit barrel.

"Nuh. All gone."

I head back into the living room. Maybe someone has left one lying round. I like Malted Milks. I like the pictures of the cows on them. They always feel a bit more substantial than say a Nice biscuit.

There's a girl on her back in the middle of the floor. Legs in the air like she just don't care. There are two other girls kissing. One too many Digestives obviously. I'd never snogged a girl before and my eyes linger on them a little too long.

"What you looking at?" says the one girl, pulling away from the other.

"Just watching." I say. The girls carry on as if I'm not there.

Just then, there's a sudden thump at the back door. The door flies open and a few girls scream. I'm not sure what's going on exactly. Something's happening. Then the music stops. Everyone stops. There is silence.

Then he speaks.

"Baaaaa!"

I'd never heard him speak before. In fact, I'd never seen him up close before. I'd only ever seen him sat on his own across the field.

I'm captivated. I can't breathe. He is beautiful.

"Baaaa!" he shouts again. This time, there is a sudden reaction from the girls. And for me, the penny drops.

Farmer Honey is on his way home. And he's just a few minutes away.

2 A THANK YOU

The sudden wave of bodies heading for the door lifts me up off my feet. I'm literally being carried up and out of the house. Before I know it, I'm back outside in the field with all the other sheep. Farmer Honey's Land Rover pulls up outside. But I know that still in the house, is that good-looking boy. I'm worried for his safety.

***

It's a few hours later and I'm stood in the field talking with the girls.

"I'm going to have to say thank you." I say.

"For what?" says Tina.

"Raising the alarm and letting us know that Farmer Honey was on his way back. He probably got into a lot of trouble for that."

"I wouldn't bother. He didn't have to do it. I think he was just using it as an excuse to perv at us girls."

"I disagree." I say. "Who is he anyway?"

"Derek. Derek the Weathersheep. Bit of an odd one. Always sat over there in the field on his own. I've never spoken to him."

I gaze over at him sat there.

"He's a bit of a looker don't you think?" I say.

"He's alright I suppose."

I spend a few minutes plucking up the courage to go and speak to him. I decide to go.

I trot off over the field. My legs are a little wobbly and my heart is all a-flutter. I keep telling myself to stay calm. As I approach, I noticed that his eyes are shut so I stop and stare.

I run my eyes down over his powerful frame. His limbs are sculpted, even at rest and sat there between his back legs are a sturdy set of large pink bollocks. He's all ram.

His eyes are closed and it's clear that he's pretending to be asleep.

"Don't pretend you're asleep." I say.

He sighs. Then he opens his eyes.

"I…we…we wanted to say thank you for

what you did back there." I say. Then he goes off on one about how he's not a hero, and that it's something that anyone would have done in that situation and that although it'd be nice to appear on the *Daily Mirror*'s 'Pride of Britain' Awards, he never really liked Piers Morgan, and in fact, he thinks Piers Morgan is a bit of an arsehole and should never have been given his own chat show after making so many people's lives a misery by hacking phones.

"Piers Morgan left the *Mirror* years ago. And it's never been proved in a court of law." I say.

"Yeah. Well. He's still a cock." says Derek. I'm taken aback by his animosity toward Piers Morgan.

"Well I just wanted to say thank you." I say and with that, I turn and head back to the girls. My heart is still skipping. He actually spoke to me! I can feel his eyes burning into me as I walk away. And it's then that I realise that I'm moist downstairs.

***

I can't sleep that night. All I can do is think of Derek who is across the other side of the barn. Why don't any of the girls like him? Or were they just in denial? Do they not know that they had a demi-god in their midst? He is a handsome sheep. And not only that, he can forecast the weather. Wow.

Later on in the day, I spot him stood high on the outcrop that looked out over the valley. He is obviously checking on the weather. What I like about him is that he is his own sheep. He doesn't need anyone to tell him what to do. He knows what he wants and he knows how to do it. I want to get to know him. As I stand there staring, he suddenly turns and our eyes meet.

Flummoxed, I pretend to half-wave and he nods back at me.

"What's the weather like today?" I shout.

"What?" comes his voice across the field.

"I said 'What's the weather like today?" I say.

"What?"

I sigh. "I said 'What's the weather like today?" I'm starting to feel stupid.

"What?"

'Jesus' I think to myself.

"Is it going to rain?"

"What?"

Ok, so this is getting a bit silly now. I can shout anything I want and he won't bloody hear me.

"Deaf bastard." I mutter under my breath.
"I'm not deaf." comes the reply.

***

Later on, I'm sat next to him and he's explaining the different cloud formations that hang in the sky.

"That one's a big rain cloud." he says but I'm not listening. My eyes are glued to his furry sheep arse. I just want to grab it and sink my teeth into it.

"And that one over there isn't a rain cloud. It's just a cloud."

"So Derek. Tell me about yourself." I say.

"What do you want to know?" he replies.

"Where you've come from. Why you don't talk to anyone else on the farm."

"I don't like other sheep." he says.

"Aw thanks." I say. It's a test.

"Nah, you're alright. The others – they just get on my tits."

"I know what you mean."

We sit there for a while without saying a word. My heart bulges at the thought that 'I'm alright'. We just sit there watching the day go by.

Derek finally breaks the silence.

"Do you fancy coming down to the

trough with me?"

"Sure."

I've never been asked out for a drink together yet here I am with possibly the handsomest sheep in the field about to go to the trough.

"I haven't got any make-up on." I say.

"You don't need it. You're pretty enough as you are."

I blush.

"And besides you wear too much lipstick. You look like Zippo the Clown."

We get up together and begin our trot to the trough. He walks very closely beside me. I can almost feel the heat from his fleece. I look around. None of the other girls have noticed that I'm with HIM. Look at me girls. Here I am with Handsomesheep.com. Everyone look at me!

We arrive at the trough.

"You first." he says. I dunk my head into the trough. The cool water soothes my tingling lips. I know he's watching me. Then he speaks.

"Nice arse. Can I mount you some time?"

3 A KISS

"Derek the Weathersheep!" I exclaim. "How dare you!" I pretend to be offended. Inside, my body is crying out to be mounted by this king of sheep.

"I'm only asking." he says. "There's no harm in that is there?"

"I'm a woman. I have feelings and emotions. Aren't you going to try and woo me first? Maybe take me out down to the bottom of the field? I'd like to get to know you better first."

I am lying.

My head spins just at the thought of his masculine sheep shape bearing down on me.

"Oh ok. Just thought you might fancy it like." he says. "There's not much else going on around here."

"Well I'm not saying no. Just don't expect me to open my legs at the drop of a hat."

"Okay." he says and wanders off back up the field. I give chase. He keeps on walking.

"Are we okay?"

"What do you mean?" he asks.

"Me and you. We're okay aren't we?"

"Yeah, course. Why?"

"I just don't want you thinking I'm a slapper."

"You're not."

"Well that's a good thing isn't it?"

"Yeah." he says. His pace doesn't slacken. "I'm off to check the weather if you don't mind." he says and heads off to the outcrop of rock in the distance. I stop and stand there in the middle of the field and sigh. I've blown my chance.

***

It's the very next day that I see him again. I'm busy eating some grass when I suddenly hear his voice behind me.

"What you doing?"

"Eating some grass."

I can sense him approaching from behind and it sends little pinpricks fizzing all over my body. I pretend not to notice. But I want it; I crave it.

'He has to be close' I say to myself. I wait. I wait for that first touch. But it doesn't come. Instead, he comes around to stand in front of me. He's looking gorgeous today. All wool and muscle. I can't stop my stomach doing somersaults.

"Want to come and see my weather charts?" he asks.

"What for?"

"You said you wanted to get to know me better."

"Okay" I say.

We head to the place where Derek likes to sit. The grass is already flattened and I sit down next to a pile of papers.

Over the next hour or so, I pretend to listen and take an interest but it all goes over my head. I can't take my eyes off his lipstick that keeps popping out and it's only a matter of time before he catches me looking.

"You looking at my sausage?"

I blush. I can do nothing but giggle. "Well it is sat there winking at me."

"Pervert." he says before pulling out another chart. I'm still smiling.

"Here. Take a look at this. It's an isobar chart. These wiggly lines here….." His voice drifts away as I lose myself in my thoughts – a heady concoction of lust and wool.

Before I know it, this Adonis of sheep is stood right in front of me. He's looking right at me with those beautiful yellow eyes and his woolly chest is puffed out.

He moves closer.

"What are you doing?" My voice cracks and he moves closer again. My heart is thumping against my ribcage, desperate to get out. My throat tightens. My legs tremble. He is inches from my face. I can smell his musky sheep smell. It fills my nostrils.

And then he kisses me.

His sheep lips, so soft, connect with mine. I close my eyes and my mind goes into a spin. I don't know where I am. But it's heavenly.

And then he pulls away. My eyes are still closed but I can feel a huge smile ripple across my face.

"You brushed your teeth this morning?" he says "You smell like a Biffa."

***

When I get back to the girls, I'm bursting to tell them. I decide not to though. I decide that I'd like to have that dirty secret in my head. When all the other girls complain about being single, I can congratulate myself on having kissed the handsomest sheep on the farm.

"What you been up to over there?" says Tina.

"Oh Derek's been showing me some weather charts."

"He's a boring git isn't he?"

"I don't think so. He's different to a lot of sheep. And he's very talented."

"Each to their own. You got any plans for the weekend? There's a new series of Take Me Out starting this Saturday."

I hadn't thought that far ahead. All I am thinking of is Derek and that kiss. It's what I think about for the next few hours and every now and then, I slip back to that moment.

The following day, I'm back with Derek. He's playing things pretty cool but inside, I'm all chewed up. I try to think up some weather-related comment.

"It hasn't rained for ages has it?"

"Seven weeks and four days now. But that's about to change. I can feel it. My charts also show a ridge of low pressure moving up from the continent which will bring some summery showers." I quiver at his mastery of all things meteorological. This man is the whole package.

Far away, over at the farm house, Farmer Honey is climbing up a ladder with a pot of paint. Round the side of the house, Mrs Honey is busy pegging out some washing on the line.

"Hm. I don't think that's a very good idea." says Derek. "He obviously hasn't checked his grazier's weather report. I'll need to let him know."

Derek rises up and heads off over the field to the house. I watch as he starts getting the attention of Farmer Honey. Derek then drags him across the field to the outcrop to show him the dark clouds gathering behind the mountains. A few seconds later, Farmer Honey is running back to the house, shouting out for Mrs Honey to get her smalls back in off the washing line.

Derek has saved the day. My hero.

He trots back to where I am sitting beaming with pride. My man. I'm very proud of him.

"We'd best head indoors. The rain isn't too far off."

We head into the barn and Derek invites me over to his patch. We settle down and it's not long before the rain starts thundering down on the roof of the barn. Surprisingly, the rest of the flock are still outside.

"They're under the old oak tree." says Derek. "It's just me and you."

My heart starts thumping. And Derek moves closer. He gently pushes me on my back and moves in to kiss me again. I can hardly breathe. Taking charge, he moves a hoof up over one of my legs. I try to speak but he simply puts a hoof on my mouth.

"Shhh…" he says and then presses his lips onto mine. The kiss is electric and I can't help myself. I grab the back of his head and lose myself in him.

He presses himself hard against me. I can feel his chipolata, now pumping up to the size of a small Greggs sausage roll, rubbing up against me.

"I want you." I say.

"I know." he says, grabbing my head and forcing it back. He's kissing my neck and I feel totally at his mercy. I'm exposed but it's thrilling me. I hadn't felt this good since Shakin' Stevens returned to the charts in 2005. He bears his weight down on me and I open my legs for him. He's grinding his hips into mine, and I thrust myself upward to meet him.

"I want to shag you," he says "I want to shag you like a sheep."

"I want you to shag me." I say, but I can hardly get the words out. I'm longing for him to have me, to take me.

"Just stick it in!" I call out. He ignores me. He teases me. His bangstick is throbbing and I reach out to grab it. It's hot.

"Stick it in me." I growl. I want him inside me now. I want him bad. But he still ignores me. It's driving me wild.

Just then, there's a long creak as the barn door slowly opens. The sound of the rain outside suddenly splashes into the barn.

"Someone's there!" I say.

"I know." says Derek, pinning me down. "That's what I was hoping for."

4 AN ARRIVAL

I'm walking on air for the following week. Derek is playing it cool as he always does and our encounter is never mentioned. Not by him anyway.

"What's the weather going to do today Dolly?" asks Tina in a sarcastic tone.

"I don't actually know." I say.

"Well you spend most of the day with the so-called weather expert. You're hardly over here with us anymore."

"Jealous are we?" I ask.

"No. Not at all." says Tina. "Will you be watching Take Me Out with HIM this weekend?"

"I'm not sure. I'll let you know." I reply and trot off to get some time away from her.

It's as I'm walking across the field that a

roar of a lorry shatters the peace. The lorry pulls up outside the farm and a tall guy gets out and knocks on the farm house door. I sit down on the grass to watch what's going on. I can see Derek watching from his place on the outcrop.

Farmer Honey comes to the door and both him and the tall guy walk around the back of the lorry. Looks like we've got a new arrival.

Off the back of the lorry comes this sheep. He's VERY handsome and stands there surveying the area like he owns the place. I'm not sure if it was because of my encounter with Derek the other day, but this sheep is giving me a throb-on. He's giving me a tingle in my dingle. God, what's happening to me? I'm becoming a bit of a nymph.

I look over to Derek. He's now sat bolt upright. He's been watching me watching this new guy. Bit of jealousy going on there?

I'm introduced to the new boy a little later in the day. He's sat talking to Tina.

"This is Dolly." she says. He casts me a glance before holding my gaze.

"And who are you?" I ask.

"His name's Juan and he's from Spain. He doesn't speak much English." says Tina on his behalf.

"I only speak da language of love." he pipes up.

"I see." I say and head on over to see Derek.

Derek isn't happy.

"Who's the new guy?" he asks.

"Some Spanish guy. Speaks the language of love apparently.

"Tosser." says Derek lifting up a chart and patting it out on the grass.

***

"It's not what it seems." says Juan in his clipped Spanish tones. I look up. I'm on the floor outside the barn, it's dark and Juan is stood over me. What is going on? Last thing I knew I was asleep inside.

"Yeah? Well go ahead. Explain away!" It's Derek's voice and he's not happy. I've got no idea what's going on.

"Well…" stutters Juan, "It's like this…erm…I've got a bolus up my arse and I was asking Dolly to take it out for me." His English clearly isn't that bad.

"A bolus? What the hell is a bolus?" bellows Derek.

"Medicine. It's up my arse."

"Is it supposed to be up there?"

"Yes. But I don't want it up there. It affects my confidence as a man."

I have to get to my feet. My heads hurts and I'm confused.

"What's going on?" I ask.

"Get over here behind me Dolly." Derek snaps. I make my way into the barn and lie back where I had been lying the last time I was awake. I can hear Derek laying down the law to Juan outside the barn and a few minutes later, he comes back in and cwtches up next to me.

"What was that all about? Why was I outside?" I ask.

"You don't want to know."

"I'd like to know seeing as I there!" I retort.

"He had his big Spanish bollocks in your face."

I didn't know whether to laugh or cry. Juan was a nice-looking specimen, don't get me wrong, but if he was going to put his bollocks in my face, it would have been nice to have been asked beforehand.

"How did I get outside the barn?"

"God knows. Come on. Get some sleep." Derek closes his eyes and lets out a deep sigh. Secretly, I'm slightly gutted that I was asleep during all of this. I wouldn't utter a word of this to Derek of course.

I wake up a few hours later. Derek is still behind me but all the other girls are out in the field.

"You awake?" I ask.

"Yes."

"How come you're not on Facebook updating the weather forecasts?"

"I'm happy here." He moves in closer behind me. I can sense he's feeling fruity. Sure enough, a few moments later, I feel his lipstick poking me in the back.

"Wanting some more are you Mr Derek?" He just lets out a groan, and grabs my hip, forcing himself closer to me. I'm ready for him to take me but there's a sudden creak as the barn door opens and in steps Juan. He looks over to where Derek and I are lying.

Without warning, Derek forces himself inside me, forcing me to squeal. He knows that Juan is watching. He's marking his territory. Derek moves his love truncheon inside me but my gaze is still fixed on Juan who stands there watching. I'm being had by one handsome sheep and I'm being watched by another. The exhilaration becomes too much and waves of lust ripple throughout my body. I want more. I push back on Derek. I want to be had. I want to be had hard. I want to be had hard by Derek the Weathersheep and I want Juan to watch.

I can't stop myself. I close my eyes as a tsunami of warm fizz rises up and spreads out from my foofer across my entire body. I'm helpless. Behind me, Derek grunts his way to his climax before letting out a big sigh.

I open my eyes. Juan has gone, leaving the barn door wide open.

"Anyone would think he was born in a barn." says Derek.

"He probably was." I say.

5 A JUMP

Derek is stood on a bale of hay in the middle of the barn.

"Girls, girls, GIRLS!" he shouts.

The murmuring soon drops to a hush while we wait for Derek to speak.

"I'd first like to thank you for coming along today." he says. "Now...as you all know, it's the Royal Welsh Show coming up in a few weeks' time. And as we all know, they do the same thing year in year out. A few cows walk around a ring and a few dogs chase sheep. I thought it was time for change. Real change. Time for us sheep to really show what we are made of. What I propose is that we put on a sky dive."

There is a bit of a commotion among the girls.

"A sky dive?" someone calls out. "How the hell are we going to do that? We've got no parachutes and no aeroplane."

"Ah. But that's where you're wrong," says Derek "We have parachutes AND we have an aeroplane."

There is another commotion among the small crowd. "But what's the point?" someone calls out.

"Because we can." replies Derek.

There is a collective groan and the girls then troupe out of the barn. There are a few mumbles of 'dickhead' and 'arsehole' as they pile out. I am the only one that's left.

"I believe in you Derek the Weathersheep." I say, looking up at him.

It is unusual for a sheep to want to do a sky-dive. But that's what I admire about Derek. He's a leader. A leader among sheep. But I can't stop thinking about Juan.

***

"I want you to be my girlfriend. Properly." says Derek.

"What do you mean?"

"Like a proper boyfriend and girlfriend. So that we buy each other Valentine's Day cards and stuff like that."

"No. I mean why do you want me to be your girlfriend?"

"You've got a nice set of teets and I don't fancy any other the other girls on the farm."

I'm not sure what Derek is up to. Why would he want to make things official? Is it because of the arrival of Juan?

"I'm not sure that I want to get too formal about things." I say. And I mean it. Being a girlfriend involves doing things like cleaning and going to Kwik Save and stuff.

"Why not?" I can tell Derek is put out. "We can go for walks down to the bottom of the field together and stuff."

"We do that anyway." I reply.

"Well we can make love instead of just bonking."

"Make love?" It's a phrase I've come to detest over the years.

"Make love? How can you 'make love'?"

"Easy. Just stick it in, tell each other that you love each other. Erm… and that's it." says Derek. I look out over the fields. I'm not sure I want a full-time boyfriend. I'd quite like to have a go at Juan if I can. Keep my options open. Derek's lovely and all that but he has turned out a bit boring. From what I know about Juan, he seems more mercurial.

"I'll think about it." I say. Derek sighs.

"What is there to think about?" he asks.

"Don't pressurise me." I say.

"I'm doing this sky-dive for you." he says.

"What do you mean?"

"To prove I'm not boring." Has he been reading my mind? What else does he know?

"Look. I think you're lovely and all that, I really do. I just don't want to rush into things in case it goes wrong and we end up losing our friendship."

"Can we still shag?"

"Yeah course."

"Lovely. That'll do." Derek rises to his feet. "Excellent. Right. I'm off for a dump." He trots off down the field and leaves me wondering. What am I doing? First, I get jiggy with Derek and now someone better-looking comes along.

Can't I have both? Sometimes, you should be careful what you wish for.

6 JEALOUSY

Derek does his jump and if I'm totally honest, it does make me feel more attracted to him. For a sheep to go up in a plane and jump out and land on all four feet (even if he was 3 miles off course) makes me think that he's a special sheep.

I treat him to some action later as a reward. For a few weeks, things are good between Derek and I. It does almost feel that we are boyfriend and girlfriend and Juan keeps his distance, leaving me to forget him a little.

But one sunny afternoon, when I'm sat in the field on my own soaking up the sun's rays, Tina comes waddling over. She's walking like John Wayne would if he was a sheep.

"What's up with you?" I ask. Tina plops down next to me.

"Just had a good seeing to from Juan behind the barn." she says.

That searing heat of jealousy rises up within me.

"He gave it to me good and proper."

"You mean you had intercourse?" I ask.

"Intercourse? Are you some kind of sex education teacher? No-one calls is that any more. But yes, there was full penetration of Juan's penis into my pelvic cavity if that's what you're asking."

"Well how did that come about?"

"He just asked if I fancied it and I said yes and off we went."

"Just like that?"

"Yes, just like that. You need to get out more Dolly love."

Tina lays back, clearly struggling with the pounding she'd taken from Juan. I feel sick. Tina's gone and tasted Juan's beef bazooka when it was all I had been thinking about up until a few weeks ago. How dare she.

"He's a big lad." says Tina.

"I don't want to know." I reply. I do, but I don't.

Tina continues. "It looked and felt like a Saturn V. There it was, sat on the launch pad. I couldn't help but sit on it. And then came the same turbulent thrusting force and energy that can send a man to the moon. Fair play to the lad. Just as a rocket can send a satellite into orbit, he sent me into orgasm, which is no less awesome a feat."

I didn't want to hear any more. I want to go find him to see what the idiot was playing at. I get up and leave Tina to her sore bits.

"Where you going?" she shouts.

"Back in a minute."

***

I find Juan relaxing at the top of the field. His eyes are closed and he has a slight smirk on his face.

"Hello Dolly." he says without opening his eyes.

"How do you know it's me?"

"I knew you'd come once Tina told you."

I'm angry. What an arrogant arsehole.

"Jealous aren't you?" I hate him. I hate his stupid accent and I hate his stupid everything.

I spin around and head back off down the field. Behind me, I hear Juan chuckling to himself.

As evening falls, Derek comes down from his rock outcrop and comes over to me. I'm sitting alone in the field. And I'm not in a good mood.

"What's the matter?" asks Derek.

"I'm fine. Nothing." He sits next to me.

"What is it?"

"Nothing. I'm fine." I've got so much anger inside me but it's not Derek's fault. I turn to him and smile. "Shall we head to the barn? The other sheep are still out in the field." Derek's face lights up.

"Excellent." he says. I'll just swill my schlong in the sheepdip. Meet you in there."

When I get to the barn, my friend Brenda's lying there next to where I would usually lie.

"You ok?" I ask.

"Yeah. Just came in for a lie down. It's too hot out there."

I lie down next to her. We both look up at the ceiling of the barn.

"What brings you in here then?" asks Brenda. Just then, Derek arrives at the barn door. He looks surprised to see me there with Brenda.

"Ahhh." says Brenda. "I get it. Well don't let me stop you two. I'm not moving." A smile wraps around Derek's face and he comes to lie down next to me.

"We can't do anything with Brenda here." I say.

"Why not?"

"Ah get on with it. I've seen it all before." says Brenda. I feel Derek run his hoof over my foof. It sends a tingle shooting up to my belly. I'm so wanting some action but I feel a little bit self-conscious with Brenda lying next to me. Derek presses his big sheep lips down onto mine.

I submit.

I wrap my front leg around the back of Derek's head and draw him in closer. He's making me tremble so much that it's registering on the Dichter Scale. His hooves are all over my lactoids.

"Kiss my butterbags." I wail. He grabs them.

"Great set of Zepplins." he says, sliding his hoof down between my legs and over my Volvo. I reach out to grab his jigger, but he holds me down and slides his woolly face down between my legs. Within seconds, he's performing tongue fu on my Beetle bonnet.

To my surprise, I feel another hoof touching my pontoons.

"Sorry." says Brenda. "I couldn't resist." I gasp as two pairs of hooves slide over my body. I'm shaking like a shitting dog. The only thing I wish for was that Juan could be here.

"Take me Derek." I cry out.

"Yes, take her." says Brenda. Derek

moves back up, his clockweights dangling between his legs. His panhandle looks glorious. Even Brenda looks on with awe.

"Didn't know you were amphibious." says Derek to Brenda.

"I do like to growl at the badger every now and then yes." she replies. "Half chips, half rice me."

I moan in ecstasy as Derek bears his weight down on me. And I'm so ready for him, it's a hole in one.

***

We're still lying there when the rest of the flock come back into the barn for the evening. Juan looks over and sees us red-faced. I smile at him and he smiles back.

"Do you fancy him?" asks Derek. He's obviously clocked us exchanging smiles.

"I don't fancy him. I think he's good-looking but I don't fancy him." I reply.

"Birrova ladies man that one, Billy Big Bollocks." says Brenda." I wouldn't go there though."

It's during the early hours of the morning when Dai the Llama burst into the barn. His night-vision goggles scan the barn.

"Everyone ok?" he says.

There are a few grumbles. From the corner of the barn comes the sound of a strangled fart.

"No riots in here then?"

No-one answers. There are a few more groans and then Dai closes the door and went back out to patrol the field.

We find out the next day that there are riots all around the country. We get a pair of goat twins to look after the farm. They're pretty hot and the rest of the girls pay them a lot of attention. But my head is already full. I'm torn. I'm going with Derek but wanting to go with Juan. Our romantic interlude with Brenda has opened my eyes to the possibility of all sorts of possibilities. Yet the two guys don't like each other much. My ultimate fantasy of being in the middle of a ram sandwich seems like a very remote possibility.

I need to sort my head out. Make a commitment. I needed to get Juan out of my mind for good. The was the plan at least until he came into the barn one day while I was alone.

7 A MONSTER

"How's your clackervalve?" Juan has entered the barn when I am alone.

"Fine thank you. How was Tina's?" I reply.

"Very good thank you." He sits next to me. "So. When can I park my pink bus in your furry garage?"

"That ain't going to happen."

"Well I can't sit around doing the Palma Sutra for the rest of my days."

"You got Tina." I say.

"Tina? You think I'll be going back there again? I don't think so."

"I'm not interested thank you."

"You're not interested in my wife-tamer?" he says. I turn to see him and am shocked to see him sat there with his stoat in his hands. It is impressive and my jaw drops.

"Don't tell me you aren't interested in this?"

I need to get away. He has had his chance but I need to get away. If not for my sake, for Derek's. But I can't take my eyes off Juan's tool. It's huge. It looks rock solid. So much so that there appears to be a miniature double of myself on it shiny head. A doppleganger dick.

"Put it away." I say but secretly, I want it. The roar of Farmer Honey's tractor pulling up outside disturbs us and Juan swiftly moves to the far side of the barn with his five legs. My face is still glowing. I can see why Tina couldn't resist. I head outside to get some fresh air.

Derek is with Dai Llama, talking tactics about how they are going to patrol the farm at night. Hoodies need to be kept away.

"You'll be on your own tonight." says Derek. "I'll be out here with Dai patrolling the field. At least you'll have Brenda to keep you company." he says and winks.

Brenda did keep me company. We had a bit of a fun while Derek was away. I couldn't stop myself. And by morning, I was still tingling. Which was awkward when Juan turned up at the trough.

"This water is horrible." he says. "Giving me stomach cramps."

"I guess you're used to Spanish water huh?"

"Yes. Over there, the water is crystal clear. This stuff is murky." he says.

"Well it's all you're going to get around here."

"What have you been up to ?" he asks. All I can think about is that image of his standing ovation.

"Nothing much. You?"

"This and that. Romancing the bone last night."

"Yeah? How is Tina?"

"Don't know." he replies. "She wasn't there."

I turn to him.

"Who was the lucky girl last night then?"

"I forget her name." His negative psychology is working. He knows what he's doing. My groins throb. I want him more than ever. Everyone else is getting a piece of that meat. I wanted to experience it.

***

It feels odd snuggling up to Derek that night. I feel comfortable around Derek and I feel that I do love him. But Juan is such a bad sheep.

"What you thinking about?" Derek asks as he cwtches me from behind.

"Just stuff."

"Oh. Good stuff I hope."

"Yea. All good ta."

As I drift off to sleep, all I can think about is Juan.

***

'It's not right' I think to myself. This shouldn't be happening. Why am I wasting so much time thinking about Juan when I have a perfectly delicious man in Derek? I feel I need to clear the air. I also think that Derek should know what's going on. If I can't be totally honest with him, then there's no point us being together.

I head up to see Derek in the field. It's another gloriously hot day but I'm nervous. How will Derek react when I tell him about my feelings for Juan?

Derek is on his new laptop, updating his friends on Facebook. He notices me arriving and looks up.

"Hiya love. You ok?"

"Yeah. Sort of. We need to talk."

"About what? You sure you're ok?"

I sit down next to him. He looks worried.

"I want you to know firstly that I like you. Really, really like you. And I think that I'm falling for you."

Derek smiles. Such a lovely sheepy smile. How can I hurt him? But he needs to know. I take a big breath.

"It's Juan. I think I'm in love with him too."

8 A PROPOSAL

"So you want to go with him too or instead of me?"

"It's not like that."

"It's exactly like that from where I'm sitting."

I sigh. "I'm just being honest with you. I do really, really like you. I guess it's more of an infatuation with him. All the girls seem to be getting in on the act and I just feel that I'm missing out."

Derek falls silent. I feel awful. I move towards him to give him a kiss but he reels away.

"I guess there's no point in carrying on this conversation." I say and get up to walk away.

"Sit down." says Derek. I sit back down.

"Look. There's something I've been meaning to tell you too." I'm confused.

Derek packs away his laptop and holds my hooves in his. He thinks hard before he speaks.

"If we're being totally honest about things, then I need to come clean too."

"Go on." I say.

"It's Brenda."

"What about her?" I ask. I feel a sudden rage building up within me.

"A few nights ago…when you were asleep…after that group thing we did…."

"What? What happened?"

"I'm sorry. I thought it was you."

"What did you do?"

"I was half asleep and she was there in front of me."

"You poked her?"

"Well not quite. I wasn't fully recovered from our session. I wasn't as hard as I would have liked. It was like playing snooker with a piece of string."

I wait for more.

"Eventually I managed to get it in but it was like packing a marshmallow in there. I thought it was you."

I'm shocked.

"I'm sorry." says Derek. I don't know

what to say. I've gone from feeling like a bitch to feeling like a woman scorned.

"Well what do we do from here?" I ask.

"If you want to make things equal, then you can go with Juan. If that makes you feel better." It's an offer only a few moments ago that I would have jumped at. But suddenly, it all seems irrelevant.

"Ok. Fine." I say. "I will." I stand up and trot off. I'm not sure if I mean it but I want Derek to feel some of my pain.

As fate would have it, the first person I bump into is Juan as he heads out into the field.

His tackle swings between his hind legs like a large bag of giblets.

"Hey. Spanish boy. You want to go with me?" I say, throwing all caution to the wind.

"Sure." he says. "When?"

"Tonight. Meet me at the top of the field."

"Lovely." he says.

***

I'm nervous as I head out to the field that night. I glance at Derek who is sitting down with Brenda in the barn. I harbour no ill-feelings towards her. I did enjoy playing her gusset piano.

The field is dark but I can make out Juan's outline against the night sky. It's a cool evening and I wonder how hot things are going to be. I look back at the barn and think of Derek. But then I picture him with his lipstick inside Brenda while I lie sleeping next to him. And I march on harder up the field.

"Good evening." he says as I approach him. I can't see him clearly but he's sat in the same position I found him in the barn that day. He was ready for me.

9 A RAM SANDWICH

We don't speak. We get straight to it. No time for choreplay. His parson's sack feels swollen. He's obviously been saving himself for me. He's working my underbeard with his hooves in advance of serving his main course. I can't wait and get my head down between his legs. I go at his bell tower like a woodpecker. And he's big. He's got the girth of a National Express coach and the length of a Thames barge. No wonder Tina was walking like John Wayne.

He begins talking in Spanish. Such a turn on. But I'm needing to get him inside me and quick. He picks me up, throws me over a nearby hay bale and drills his spam javelin inside me. I feel like I'm being torn in two.

He grabs me by the back of the head and

lifts it up.

"Looks like we've got company." he says. I peer into the darkness. I can't see anything. I try to speak but I'm having all the air in my lungs banged out of me.

"And it looks like it's your man." I look again. Sure enough, looming out of the darkness is Derek.

"Come to watch?" calls Juan. I hear Derek's voice call back.

"No. I've come to join in." The thought sends me wild. Before I know it, Derek is stood right in front of me. His soldier of love is just inches from my mouth.

"You're very welcome." says Juan. I get little say in the matter. I can hardly speak.

"To me." says Derek.

"To you." replies Juan.

"Let Percy in the playpen." I'm beginning to lose all sense of everything. All I know is, is that I'm being taken from both ends by the Chuckle Brothers. And I'm loving it.

They swap ends. I hardly get a moment to breathe before Juan opens my mouth and fills it with his thunder-rod.

But then it all goes wrong. Derek is going at me from behind like the clappers. But Juan pulls out.

"I'm sorry." he says. "I've got a grumbling

stomach. It must be the water round here. It's making me ill."

With that, he holds his stomach and lets out a shot gun fart which peppers pellets of crapnel into a small pile on the floor by his hooves.

"I'm sorry, I'm so sorry." he says. He clutches his stomach again and now floats an air biscuit right into my face.

I feel sick. Juan runs off down the field, clutching his stomach and still parping.

"Well." says Derek. "Shall I finish you off?"

"Yes please." I say.

10 MY MAN

The next day, Juan keeps himself to himself. Every time I see him, I get a warm waft of sheep shit in my nostrils. Derek is back in the field, checking his charts. I head over to him.

"Are we even Stevens now?" I say, taking my place next to him.

"Aye. I guess so." he says. "You know, I know that you love me and I also know that there are other good-looking men out there. I can't compete with all of them. As long as I'm the one you love, I don't mind you looking."

"Aw. And do you mind me going with them?" I say.

"As long as we're all in the same room." he replies. "I'd feel a bit greedy keeping you all to myself."

I sit back and look over the fields. The

sun is scorching the fields in the valley below but a cool breeze flutters over us.

"We're going to have a great summer aren't we Derek the Weathersheep?" I say.

"Yes Dolly. We are."

ABOUT THE AUTHOR

Derek The Weathersheep lives on a Rex Honey's Farm high in the Brecon Beacons, South Wales.

From his high vantage point, Derek can cast his sheep's eye across the whole of South Wales, and forecast the South Walian population about forth-coming weather events.

He first caught the meteorological bug when he was just a lamb. He was the first sheep to correctly forecast the great snows of 2006, when he ran to Farmer Honey's house, woke him from his slumber, bleated for a bit, and then led Farmer Honey to the rest of the sheep who were about to be cut off from the farm by the drifts. 48 sheep were rescued that night. Farmer Honey rewarded him by presenting him with the Freedom of Honey Farm.

Derek's girlfriend, Dolly (not to be confused with the famous cloned one- they just look alike) is the best looking ewe on the field, and constantly draws attention from male sheep and sometimes even other female sheep. Juan the LoveSheep, a Spanish import, brought by Farmer Honey, to increase virility in the flock, constantly tries to woo Dolly, much to Derek's dismay and amusement.

More books are available at www.weathersheep.com

23755934R00033

Printed in Great Britain
by Amazon